SPURGEON'S VERSE EXPOSITION OF GALAT.

By Charles H. Spurgeon

ISBN: 9781521384640

May 2017

Charles H. Spurgeon's Galatians Commentary Contents

<u>Galatians Chapter 1</u>

Verses 1-24

Galatians 1:1. Paul, an apostle, (not of men, neither by man, but by Jesus Christ, and God the Father, who raised him from the dead;) —

Paul begins this Epistle by stating his commission as an apostle. In Galatia, he had been subjected to the great sorrow of having his apostle-ship called in question. Does he, therefore, give up his claim to the office, and retire from the work? No, not for a moment; but he begins his letter to the Galatians by declaring himself to be "an apostle, not of men, neither by man, but by Jesus Christ." His enemies had said, "Paul was never one of the Saviour's twelve apostles; he is not like those who were trained and educated by Christ himself. No doubt he has borrowed his doctrine from them, and he is only a retailer of other men's goods". No, no," says Paul, "I am an apostle as truly as any other of the twelve; 'not of men, neither by man, but by Jesus Christ, and God the Father, who raised him from the dead;'" —

Galatians 1:2. And all the brethren which are with me, unto the churches of Galatia: —

Paul ever loved to associate others with him in his Christian service. He was not one who wanted to ride the high horse, and to keep himself aloof from his brethren in Christ. He frequently mentions the true-hearted men who were with him, even though they were far inferior to him in talent and also in grace. He often joins with himself such men as Timothy and Silvanus, and here he puts in, "all the brethren which are with me, unto the churches of Galatia:" —

Galatians 1:3. Grace be to you and peace from God the Father, and from our Lord Jesus Christ, —

It is the genius of the gospel to wish well to others. Hence Paul begins the actual Epistle with a benediction: "Grace be to you and peace." Dear friends, may you all have a fullness of these two good things! Grace rightly comes first, and peace afterwards. Peace before grace would be perilous; nay more, it would be ruinous. But may you always have enough of grace to lead you on to a deep and joyful peace! The two things go together very delightfully, — grace and peace, — and it is the best of grace, and the best of peace, since they come "from God the Father, and from our Lord Jesus Christ," —

Galatians 1:4. Who gave himself for our sins, —

There is the doctrine of the atonement, which Paul always brings into his preaching and writing as soon as he can: "Who gave himself for our sins." Well does Luther say, "Christ never gave himself for our righteousness; but he gave himself for our sins, because there was no other way of saving us except by a sacrifice for sin." The substitutionary character of Christ's death is always to be noticed: "Who gave himself for our sins," —

Galatians 1:4-5. That he might deliver us from this present evil world, according to the will of God and our Father: to whom be glory for ever and ever. Amen.

Our Lord Jesus Christ himself puts away our sin in order that we may rise out of it, and may become a pure and holy people, delivered from this present evil world, and brought into obedience to the will of God. Now we come to quite another topic.

Galatians 1:6. I marvel that ye are so soon removed from him that called you into the grace of Christ unto another gospel:

The Galatians were a very fickle people. Some have said that they were a colony from Gaul, — Galatians, — and that they partook somewhat of the fickleness which is attributed to the character of the Gaul. I know not how true that may be; but, certainly, they seem very soon to have left the gospel, to have adulterated it, and to have fallen into Ritualism, into Sacramentarianism, into salvation by works, and all the errors into which people usually fall when they go away from the gospel.

Galatians 1:7. Which is not another; but there be some that trouble you, and would pervert the gospel of Christ.

"Another gospel: which is not another;" for there are not two gospels, any more than there are two gods. There is one only message from God, of good news to men; and if you turn away from that, you turn away to a falsehood, to that which will bring you trouble, to that which will pervert you, and lead you astray.

Galatians 1:8. But though we, or an angel from heaven, preach any other gospel unto you than that which we have preached unto you, let him be accursed.

Paul is no fanatic, no raving enthusiast; yet he cannot endure the notion of a false gospel. In his solemn anathema, he includes himself, and all the brethren with him, yea, and the very angels of God if they "preach any other gospel." Let him be accursed, saith he, and so he is.

Galatians 1:9. As we said before, so say I now again, If any man preach any other gospel unto you than that ye have received, let him be accursed.

The modern style of speaking is, "Let us fraternize with him; he is a man of original thought. Surely, you would not bind all men down to one mode of speech. Perhaps, if he has made mistakes, you will bring him round to your way of thinking By receiving him kindly into your fellowship." "No, no;" says Paul, "As we said before, so say I now again, If any man preach any other gospel unto you than that ye have received, let him be accursed."

Galatians 1:10. For do I now persuade men, or God? or do I seek to please men? for if I yet pleased men, I should not be the servant of Christ.

He would not be the servant of Christ if he pleased men. Those whom we try to please, are our masters. If a man tries to please the populace, or to please the refined few, these are his masters, and he will be their flare; but if he tries to please his God, then is he a free man indeed.

Galatians 1:11-12. But I certify you, brethren, that the gospel which was preached of me is not after man. For I neither received it of man, neither was I taught it, but by the revelation of Jesus Christ.

Paul foresaw what would be said about him in the after ages; and truly, to this day, the fiercest attack upon Christianity is always made upon the teaching of the apostle Paul. The men who creep in unawares among us talk glibly about having great reverence for Christ, but none for Paul. Yet Paul is Christ's apostle; Paul speaks only what was personally revealed to him by the Lord himself; and he is in everything to be accepted as speaking by divine revelation.

Galatians 1:13-14. For ye have heard of my conversation in time past in the Jews' religion, how that beyond measure I persecuted the church of God, and wasted it: and profited in the Jews' religion above many my equals in mine own nation, being more exceedingly zealous of the traditions of my fathers.

He was an out-and-out Jew. He never took up anything without going through with it thoroughly; so, while he believed in Judaism, he did believe it. He was no hypocrite, no pretender, so he fought for it tooth and nail. This was the man who afterwards preached the Christianity he had received from Christ, Evidently he did not borrow it from his parents, for they had taught him quite differently. His religion was not the product of his training; but it came to him from God, — to him who seemed to be the most unlikely person in the whole land ever to receive it.

Galatians 1:15-16. But when it pleased God, who separated me from my mother's womb, and called me by his grace, to reveal his Son in me, that I might preach him among the heathen; immediately I conferred not with flesh and blood:

He felt divinely called to preach the gospel Christ revealed himself to him on the way to Damascus. As soon as he was converted, he did not wait for anybody to ordain him, or to teach him further, but he says, "I conferred not with flesh and blood"

Galatians 1:17. Neither went I up to Jerusalem to them which were apostles before me, but went into Arabia, —

What he did there, we do not know; but probably he had a time of quiet meditation and prayer, all alone: "I went into Arabia." The best thing we can do, sometimes, is to get away from the voices of men, and listen only to the voice of God: "I went into Arabia," —

Galatians 1:17. And returned again unto Damascus.

To bear witness for Christ in the very city where he had gone to persecute the saints.

Galatians 1:18. Then after three years I went up to Jerusalem to see Peter, and abode with him fifteen days.

That is, "after three years," which showed that he did not go there to receive any commission from Peter. He had been for three years working for his Lord and Master before he ever saw the face of an apostle.

Galatians 1:19. But other of the apostles saw I none, save James the Lord's brother.

He had an interview with the apostle James. He was probably the chief minister of the church at Jerusalem, so Paul went and had a conversation with him.

Galatians 1:20. Now the things which I write unto you, behold, before God, I lie not.

"I did not derive my knowledge of Christ from any one of these holy men, therefore I am not an imitator of any other apostle. I was sent out by Christ himself, and instructed by him by revelation, so I am an apostle of Christ as much as any of them."

Galatians 1:21-22. Afterwards I came into the regions of Syria, and Cilicia; and was unknown by face unto the churches of Judaea which were in Christ:

They did not know him; it is evident that he had not been there to be taught by them, or else they would have recognized their illustrious pupil.

Galatians 1:23-24. But they had heard only, That he which persecuted us in times past now preacheth the faith which once he destroyed. And they glorified God in me.

Brothers and sisters, may you and I so live that Christian people may glorify God in us! May they often wonder at the mighty grace which has wrought such a change in us; and as they see us zealous and fervent, may they marvel at the amazing grace of God which has brought us to be so consecrated to Christ!

Verses 11-24

Galatians 1:11-17. But I certify you, brethren, that the gospel that was preached of me is not after man. For I neither received it of man, neither was I taught it, but the revelation of Jesus Christ. For ye have heard of my conversation in time past in the Jews' religion, how that beyond measure I persecuted the church of God, and wasted it: and profited in the Jews' religion above many my equals in mine own nation, being more exceedingly jealous of the traditions of my fathers. But when it pleased God, who separated me from my mother's womb, and called me by his grace, to reveal his Son in me, that I might preach him among the heathen; immediately I conferred not with flesh and blood: neither went I up to Jerusalem to them which were apostles before me; but I went up to Arabia, and returned again unto Damascus.

Paul was intensely desirous that the Galatian Christians should understand that he was no mere repeater of other men's doctrines, but that what he taught he had received directly from God by supernatural revelation. They knew that he had been a most determined opposer of the gospel. Indeed, he was a man of such great determination that, whatever he did he did with all his might; so, no sooner did God reveal Christ to him, so that he knew Jesus to be the Messiah, than he earnestly sought to learn yet more of the truth, not by going up to the apostles at Jerusalem, to borrow from them, but by getting alone in the waste places of Arabia? there, by thought and meditation upon the Word, and by communion with God, to learn yet more concerning the divine mysteries.

Galatians 1:18-24. Then after three years I went to Jerusalem to see Peter, and abode with him fifteen days. But other of the apostles saw I none, save James the Lord's brother. Now the things which I write unto you, behold, before God, I lie not. Afterwards I came into the regions of Syria and Cilicia; and was unknown by face unto the churches of Judaea which were in Christ: but they had heard only, That he which persecuted us in times past now preacheth the faith which once he destroyed. And they glorified God in me.

This exposition consisted of readings from Galatians 1:11-24; Galatians 2.

Galatians Chapter 2

Verses 1-21

Galatians 2:1-2. Then fourteen years after I went up again to Jerusalem with Barnabas, and took Titus with me also. And I went up by revelation,-

He was sent by the church at Antioch, but the church there was guided by revelation, so that Paul is correct in saying, "I went up by revelation," —

Galatians 2:2-4. And communicated unto them that gospel which I preach among the Gentiles, but privately to them which were of reputation, lest by any means I should run, or had run, in vain. But neither Titus, who was with me, being a Greek, was compelled to be circumcised: and that because of false brethren unawares brought in, who came in privily to spy out our liberty which we have in Christ Jesus, that they might bring us into bondage:

There were always some among the Jewish converts who insisted that the Gentiles should come under the seal of the old covenant if they were to be partakers of the blessings of the gospel, but to this Paul would never consent: —

Galatians 2:5. To whom we gave place by subjection, no, not for an hour; that the truth of the gospel might continue with you.

It is impossible for us to estimate how much we owe to the apostle Paul. Of all who have ever lived, we who are Gentiles owe more to him than to any other man. See how he fought our battles for us. When our Jewish brethren would have excluded us because we were not of the seed of Abraham according to the flesh, how bravely did he contend that, if we were partakers of the same faith, Abraham is the father of all the faithful that he was loved of God, and the covenant was made with him, not in circumcision, but before he was circumcised, and that we are partakers of that covenant.

Galatians 2:6-10. But of these who seemed to be somewhat, (whatsoever they were, it maketh no matter to me: God accepteth no man's person:) for they who seemed to be somewhat in conference added nothing to me: but contrawise, when they saw that the gospel of the uncircumcision was committed unto me, as the gospel of the circumcision was unto Peter; (for he wrought effectually in Peter to the apostleship of the circumcision, the same was mighty to me toward the Gentiles:) and when James, Cephas, and John, who seemed to be pillars, perceived the grace that was given unto me, they gave to me and Barnabas the right hands of fellowship; that we should go unto the heathen, and they unto the circumcision. Only they would that we should remember the poor; the same which I also was forward to do.

One of the first things he did, when there was a famine in Judaea, was to make a collection for the saints in other places, that he might aid the poor Christians.

Galatians 2:11-14. But when Peter was come to Antioch, I withstood him to the face, because he was to be blamed. For before that certain came from James, he did eat with the Gentiles: but when they were come, he withdrew and separated himself, fearing them which were of the circumcision. And the other Jews dissembled likewise with him; insomuch that Barnabas also was carried away with their dissimulation. But when I saw that they walked not uprightly according to the truth of the gospel, I said unto Peter before them all, If thou, being a Jew, livest after the manner of Gentiles, and not as do the Jews, why compellest thou the Gentiles to live as do the Jews?

It must have been very painful to Paul's feelings to come into conflict with Peter, whom he greatly esteemed; but yet, for the truth's sake, he knew no persons, and he had to withstand even a beloved brother when he saw that he was likely to pervert the simplicity of the gospel, and rob the Gentiles of their Christian liberty. For this, we ought to be very grateful to our gracious God who raised up this brave champion, this beloved apostle of the Gentiles.

Galatians 2:15-16. We who are Jews by nature, and not sinners of the Gentiles, knowing that a man is not justified by the works of the law, but by the faith of Jesus Christ, even we have believed in Jesus Christ, that we might be justified by the faith of Christ, and not by the works of the law: for by the works of the law shall no flesh be justified.

No mere man can keep the law; no mere man has ever done so. We have all sinned, and come short of the glory of God; and as an absolutely perfect obedience is demanded by the law, which knows nothing of mercy we fly from the law to obtain salvation by the grace of God in Christ Jesus

Galatians 2:17. But if, while we seek to be justified by Christ, we ourselves also are found sinners, is therefore Christ the minister of sin? God forbid.

That would not be caused by the gospel, but by our disregard of it.

Galatians 2:18-19. For if I build again the things which I destroyed, I make myself a transgressor. For I through the law am dead to the law, that I might live unto God.

"Through my sight of the law, which I have seen to be so stern that all it call do is to condemn me for my shortcomings, I am driven away from it, and led to come and live in Christ Jesus, under the rule of grace, and not under the law of Moses."

Galatians 2:20-21. I am crucified with Christ: nevertheless I live; yet not I, but Christ liveth in me: and the life which I now live in the flesh I live by the faith of the Son of God, who loved me, and gave himself for me. I do not frustrate the grace of God: for if righteousness come by the law, then Christ is dead in vain.

This exposition consisted of readings from Galatians 1:11-24; Galatians 2.

Verses 15-21

Galatians 2:15-21. We who are Jews by nature, and not sinners of the Gentiles, knowing that a man is not justified by the works of the law, but by the faith of Jesus Christ, even we have believed in Jesus Christ, that we might be justified by the faith of Christ, and not by the works of the law: for by the works of the law shall no flesh be justified. But if, while we seek to be justified by Christ, we ourselves also are found sinners, is therefore Christ the minister of sin? God forbid. For if I build again the things which I destroyed, I make myself a transgressor. For I through the law am dead to the law, that I might live unto God. I am crucified with Christ: nevertheless I live; yet not I, but Christ liveth in me: and the life which I now live in the flesh I live by the faith of the Son of God, who loved me, and gave himself for me. I do not frustrate the grace of God: for if righteousness come by the law, then Christ is dead in vain.

Paul is arguing against the idea of salvation by works, or salvation by ceremonies; and he shows, beyond all question, that salvation is by the grace of God through faith in Jesus Christ. Mark the strength of the apostle's argument in the 21st verse: " If righteousness come by the law, then Christ is dead in sin." That is to say, there was no need for Christ to die, the crucifixion was a superfluity, if men can save themselves by their own good works. Paul is very emphatic about the matter. He puts it as plainly as possible: "If righteousness come by the law, then Christ is dead in vain."

This exposition consisted of readings from Galatians 2:15-21; Galatians 3.

Verses 16-21

Galatians 2:16. Knowing that a man is not justified by the works of the law, but by the faith of Jesus Christ, even we have believed in Jesus Christ, that we might be justified by the faith of Christ, and not by the works of the law: for by the works of the law shall no flesh be justified.

This is the primary truth to be proclaimed by the Christian ministry. It is the foundation-stone of all gospel preaching; and yet, somehow or other, such is the hardness of the human heart, that it is the most difficult thing to induce our hearers to build on this foundation. Many of them are always trying to lean upon their own works, and so struggling to get back under the old legal dispensation, instead of rejoicing in the liberty of the dispensation of grace. One objection to the doctrine of grace rather than the doctrine of law is this, that some think it will lead to sin. The apostle puts it thus: —

Galatians 2:17. But if, while we seek to be justified by Christ, we ourselves also are found sinners, is therefore Christ the minister of sin? God forbid.

For the tendency of the gospel of grace is to excite gratitude in those who receive it. If I am freely pardoned, then I must love him who has thus generously forgiven me. Gratitude is the root of true virtue, and the main-spring of all holiness. If there be base-minded men who can suck poison out of this honeycomb, is Christ to be blamed for their evil-doing? God forbid! But if, on the other hand, you and I go back to trusting in works, then we are indeed guilty in the sight of God.

Galatians 2:18. For if I build again the things which I destroyed, I make myself a transgressor.

If I once said I would not trust in my good works, and now go back to trust in them, I have already, whatever may be my outward conduct, perpetrated a great sin.

Galatians 2:19-20. For I through the law am dead to the law, that I might live unto God. I am crucified with Christ: nevertheless I live; yet not I, but Christ liveth in me: and the life which I now live in the flesh I live by the faith of the Son of God, who loved me, and gave himself for me.

I do not know a better epitome of Christian experience than this. This is the daily walk of a true child of God, if he liveth after any other sort, then he liveth not a Christian's life at all. Christ living in us, ourselves living upon Christ, and our union to Christ being visibly maintained by an act of simple faith in him, this is the true Christian's life.

Galatians 2:21. I do not frustrate the grace of God: for if righteousness come by the law, then Christ is dead in vain.

If a man can be saved by his own works, and willings, and doings, then Christ's death was an unnecessary piece of torture; and, instead of being the most glorious manifestation of divine love, it was a shameful waste, putting upon Christ a terrible burden of suffering which was totally unnecessary.

This exposition consisted of readings from Galatians 2:16-21; Galatians 2:3.

Galatians Chapter 3

Verses 1-29

Galatians 3:1. O foolish Galatians, who hath bewitched you, that ye should not obey the truth, before whose eyes Jesus Christ hath been evidently set forth, crucified among you?

These Galatians thought that they were very philosophical, and very intellectual; but the apostle says, "O foolish Galatians!" They thought that they had been led by reason, and guided by the learning of their teachers; but Paul calls it witchery: "Who hath bewitched you?" he asks, as if anything which led a man to trust in his own works should be as much abhorred as the incantations of a witch, "Who hath bewitched you?" It is a dangerous state, it is a devilish snare to be brought into; to be led to trust to frames, and feelings, and experiences, and doings, and prayings, or to anything else but Christ. It is a strange thing that those who have seen Christ should ever go back to these things. Lord, keep us every day, amongst our other sins, from our own self-righteous nature!
Now the apostle is going to reason with the Galatians against their self-righteousness.

Galatians 3:2. This only would I learn of you, Received ye the Spirit by the works of the law, or by the hearing of faith?

"You know that the Spirit of God is necessary to salvation. You have received that; did you get the Spirit through the works of the law, or by simply hearing the gospel, and believing it?" The answer comes at once if we have received the Spirit, it was by the hearing of faith, and not by the works of the law.

Galatians 3:3. Are ye so foolish? having begun in the Spirit, are ye now made perfect by the flesh?

Surely, the way in which the Christian life begins is the method in which it is to be sustained. "As ye have received Christ Jesus, the Lord," the apostle says in another place, "so walk ye in him." If you have begun in the flesh, go on in the flesh, but if you really know that your beginning was in the Spirit, then go not back to the flesh.

Galatians 3:4. Have ye suffered so many things in vain? if it be yet in vain.

This is another pertinent question.

Galatians 3:5. He therefore that ministereth to you the Spirit, and worketh miracles among you, doeth he it by the works of the law, or by the hearing of faith?

They had miraculous gifts among them as a church, and the apostle asks them whether these were works of the law, or whether they were not exercised as the result of faith. The answer is clear. It was the believing man who wrought the miracle, not the self-righteous man. Paul is now going to take the Galatians far back in Jewish history.

Galatians 3:6. Even as Abraham believed God, and it was accounted to him for righteousness.

He was not saved by his works, but by his faith. His faith was the means of the imputation to him of the righteousness of the Saviour who was yet to come.

Galatians 3:7. Know ye therefore that they which are of faith, the same are the children of Abraham.

He was called the father of the faithful, therefore the faithful, those who believe as he did, and are full of his faith, are his children.

Galatians 3:8-10. And the scripture, foreseeing that God would justify the heathen through faith, preached before the gospel unto Abraham, saying, In thee shall all nations be blessed. So then they which be of faith are blessed with faithful Abraham. For as many as are of the works of the law are under the curse: for it is written, Cursed is every one that continueth not in all things which are written in the book of the law to do them.

Now, if every one who has once violated God's law is cursed for ever, how mad are those who hope to enter heaven by that very law which is the gate to shut them out! How dare they confide in that which is their worst enemy, which is sworn to curse them, in time and in eternity?

Galatians 3:11. But that no man is justified by the law in the sight of God, it is evident: for, The just shall live by faith.

Scripture lays it down as a rule, that justified men live by faith; if this be the rule, then certainly they do not live by works.

Galatians 3:12. And the law is not of faith: but, The man that doeth them shall live in them.

So that the justified man is not justified by the law, but by faith. He standeth before God, not in what he does, not even in what the Spirit enables him to do; his own prayers, and tears, and communings with Christ, his own labours, his earnest and indefatigable attempts to extend the kingdom of Christ, all tell for nothing in the matter of his justification. He hangeth them all upon the cross of Christ, and relieth only upon the cross, looking in no manner whatever to anything which cometh of himself.

Galatians 3:13-14. Christ hath redeemed us from the curse of the law, being made a curse for us: for it is written, Cursed is every one that hangeth on a tree: that the blessing of Abraham might come on the Gentiles through Jesus Christ; that we might receive the promise of the Spirit through faith.

We were all under the curse of the law, but Christ voluntarily took our place, and was made a curse for us, so that the blessing might be ours.

Galatians 3:15-16. Brethren, I speak after the manner of men; Though it be but a man's covenant, yet if it be confirmed, no man disannulleth, or addeth thereto. Now to Abraham and his seed were the promises made. He saith not, And to seeds, as of many; but as of one, And to thy seed, which is Christ.

Notice how important a single letter of the Scriptures may be. If vital doctrine may depend upon the use of a singular or plural noun, therefore let us jealously guard the smallest jot or tittle of the inspired Word of God.

Galatians 3:17-19. And this I say, that the covenant, that was confirmed before of God in Christ, the law, which was four hundred and thirty years after, cannot disannul, that it should make the promise of none effect. For if the inheritance be of the law, it is no more of promise: but God gave it to Abraham by promise. Wherefore then serveth the law?

Some might argue that, as the law cannot justify, it is useless, but, on the contrary, it serves a very definite purpose, as Paul goes on to show.

Galatians 3:19-22. It was added because of transgressions, till the seed should come to whom the promise was made; and it was ordained by angels in the hand of a mediator. Now a mediator is not a mediator of one, but God is one. Is the law then against the promises of God? God forbid: for if there had been a law given which could have given life, verily righteousness should have been by the law. But the scripture hath concluded all under sin, that the promise by faith of Jesus Christ might be given to them that believe.

Paul constantly comes back to this point, that salvation is all of grace, through faith in Jesus Christ.

Galatians 3:23-25. But before faith came, we were kept under the law, shut up unto the faith which should afterward be revealed. Wherefore the law was our schoolmaster to bring us unto Christ, that we might be justified by faith. But after that faith is come, we are no longer under a schoolmaster.

The apostle is not speaking of a schoolmaster, as we understand that word; but of the slave or servant who took the boys to school, watched over them in school and out, and even used the rod if occasion demanded.

Galatians 3:26. For ye are all the children of God by faith in Christ Jesus.

The fatherhood of God is common to all believers; but there is no universal fatherhood, as many teach it in these days.

Galatians 3:27-29. For as many of you as have been baptized into Christ have put on Christ. There is neither Jew nor Greek, there is neither bond nor free, there is neither male nor female: for ye are all one in Christ Jesus. And if ye be Christ's, then are ye Abraham's seed, and heirs according to the promise.

May this be true of all of us, for Christ's sake! Amen.

This exposition consisted of readings from Galatians 2:16-21; Galatians 2:3.

<u>Galatians Chapter 4</u>

Verses 1-31

Galatians 4:1-5. Now I say, That the heir, as long as he is a child, differeth nothing from a servant, though he be lord of all; but is under tutors and governors until the time appointed of the father. Even so we, when we were children, were in bondage under the elements of the world: but when the fullness of the time was come, God sent forth his Son, made of a woman, made under the law, to redeem them that were under the law, that we might receive the adoption of sons.

Like little children, the Jewish believers were under the law. They observed this ceremony and that, just as children, even though they may be heirs to vast estates, yet, while they are in their minority, are under tutors and governors. But now in Christ we have come of age, and we have done with those school-books and that tutorship, and we have received the adoption of sons. Now, we have joy and peace in believing; we have begun to enter into our possession; we have the earnest of it already, and by-and-by we shall receive the fullness of the inheritance of the saints in light.

Galatians 4:6. And because ye are sons, God hath sent forth the Spirit of his Son into your hearts, crying, Abba, Father.

While the Jewish believers, like children, were under the law, they did not have such direct access to the Father as we have. They could not enter into such close fellowship with God as now we can. We who are the sons of God, really born into his family, feel within us a something that makes us call God, "Father," not only in prayer, saying, "Our Father, which art in heaven;" but, inwardly, when we are not in the attitude of prayer, our hearts keep on crying, "Father, Father." The Jew may say, "Abba, and the word is very sweet; but we cry, "Father," and it means the same thing.

Galatians 4:7. Wherefore thou art no more a servant, but a son; and if a son, then an heir of God through Christ.

All God's sons are, in a certain sense, his servants; but there is a sense in which servants are not sons. We, therefore, are not like those servants who have no relationship to their master, and no share in his possessions; but we are sons. Whatever service we render, we are still sons, and we have a share in all that our Father has; we are heirs, "heirs of God, and joint-heirs with Christ." Are you living up to your privileges, brethren? Are we any of us fully realizing what this heirship means? Do we not often live as if we were only servants toiling for hire? Do we not tremble at God as if we were his slaves rather than his sons? Let us remember that we are God's sons, his heirs; and let us come close to him, let us take possession of the blessed inheritance which he has provided for us.

Galatians 4:8-11. Howbeit then, when ye knew not God, ye did service unto them which by nature are no gods. But now, after that ye have known God, or rather are known of God, how turn ye again to the weak and beggarly elements, whereunto ye desire again to be in bondage? Ye observe days, and months, and times, and years. I am afraid of you, lest I have bestowed upon you labour in vain.

Among the heathen, there were divers "lucky" and "unlucky" days; sacred days, and days in which they indulged in sensual excess. They had even "holy" months and "unholy" months. Now, all that kind of thing is done away with in the case of a Christian: he is set free from such weak and beggarly superstitions. Among the Jews, there were certain sacred festivals, times that were more notable than other seasons; but they also were done away with in Christ. We observe the Christian Sabbath; but beyond that, to the true believer, there should be no special observance of days, and months, and years. All that is a return to "the weak and beggarly elements" from which Christ has delivered him. That bondage is all ended now; but there are some who still "observe days, and months, and times, and years;" and Paul says to them, "I am afraid of you, lest I have bestowed upon you labour in vain." Every day is holy, every year is holy, to a holy man; and every place is holy, too, to the man who brings a holy heart into it.

Galatians 4:12. Brethren, I beseech you, be as I am; for I am as ye are: ye have not injured me at all.

"Be perfectly at home with me, for I am so with you. Though you Galatians have treated me very badly, yet ye have not really injured me, and I freely overlook your ill manners toward me."

Galatians 4:13-15. Ye know how through infirmity of the flesh I preached the gospel unto you at the first. And my temptation which was in my flesh ye despised not, nor rejected; but received me as an angel of God, even as Christ Jesus. Where is then the blessedness ye spake of? for I bear you record, that, if it had been possible, ye would have plucked out your own eyes, and have given them to me.

The apostle remembers how they received him at first, his gospel was to them like life from the dead; and though he was full of infirmities, —perhaps had weak eyes, — perhaps had a stammering tongue, — perhaps was at that time very much depressed in spirit, — yet, he says, "You received me as an angel of God, even as Christ Jesus. You loved me so much that, if it had been possible, you would have plucked out your own eyes, and have given them to me."

Galatians 4:16. Am I therefore become your enemy, because I tell you the truth?

There come times, with all God's servants, when certain people proclaim something fresh and new in doctrine; and then the old messenger of God, who was blessed to them, comes to be despised. I have lived long enough to see dozens of very fine fancies started, but they have all come to nothing; I daresay I shall see a dozen more, and they will all come to nothing. But here I stand; I am not led astray either by novelties of excitement or novelties of doctrine. The things which I preached at the first, I preach still, and so I shall continue, as God shall help me. But I know, in some little measure, what the apostle meant when he said, "Am I therefore become your enemy, because I tell you the truth?"

Galatians 4:17-20. They zealously affect you, but not well; yea, they would exclude you, that ye might affect them. But it is good to be zealously affected always in a good thing, and not only when I am present with you. My little children, of whom I travail in birth again until Christ be formed in you, I desire to be present with you now, and to change my voice; for I stand in doubt of you.

The point of doubt was, that they had been led astray by legal teachers; they had been made to believe that, after all, there was something in outward ceremonies, something in the works of the law, and so they had come under bondage again. So the apostle says, —

Galatians 4:21-23. Tell me, ye that desire to be under the law, do ye not hear the law? For it is written, that Abraham had two sons, the one by a bondmaid, the other by a free woman. But he who was of the bondwoman was born after the flesh; —

By Abraham's own strength; —

Galatians 4:23. But he of the freewoman was by promise.

Born when Abraham and his wife were past age, — born by the power of God's Spirit, according to promise.

Galatians 4:24. Which things are an allegory: for these are the two covenants: the one from the mount Sinai, which gendereth to bondage, which is Hagar.

It is the strength of the flesh which leads to bondage.

Galatians 4:25-26. For this Hgar is mount Sinai in Arabia, and answereth to Jerusalem which now is, and is in bondage with her children. But Jerusalem which is above is free, which is the mother of us all.

That is, of all of us who believe in Christ Jesus. We are born of the free-woman, not of the bondwoman; not born of the covenant of works, and in the strength of the creature; but born of the covenant of grace, in the power of God, according to promise.

Galatians 4:27-28. For it is written, Rejoice, thou barren that bearest not; break forth and cry, thou that travailest not: for the desolate hath many more children than she which hath an husband. Now we, brethren, as Isaac was, are the children of promise.

If we are God's children, it is not by our own strength, or by the strength of the flesh, in any measure or degree; but it is by the grace of God, and the promise of God, that we are what we are.

Galatians 4:29-30. But as then he that was born after the flesh persecuted him that was born after the Spirit, even so it is now. Nevertheless what saith the scripture?

Make a compromise, and be friends? Let Isaac and Ishmael live in the same house, and lie in the same bed? No!

Galatians 4:30-31. Cast out the bondwoman and her son: for the son of the bondwoman shall not be heir with the son of the freewoman. So then, brethren, we are not children of the bondwoman, but of the free.

Galatians 5:1. Stand fast therefore in the liberty wherewith Christ hath made us free, and be not entangled again with the yoke of bondage.

God grant us grace to keep to grace! God grant us faith enough to live by faith, even to the end, as the freeborn children of God, for his name's sake! Amen.

Verses 12-31

Galatians 4:12. Brethren, I beseech you, be as I am; for I am as ye are: ye have not injured me at all.

He had told them the gospel, and other teachers had come in and alienated their affections. He says, "Now I am just the same to you as ever I was; I wish you would have the same love to me."

Galatians 4:13-14. Ye know how through infirmity of the flesh I preached the gospel unto you at the first. And my temptation which was in my flesh ye despised not, nor rejected; but received me as an angel of God, even as Christ Jesus.

He dwells upon that. They had been so enthusiastic about his teaching when he first taught them, that he feels grieved that now they have gone aside to other teaching — not because it injured him, but because it injured them.

Galatians 4:15. Where is then the blessedness ye spake of?

When you said that you were happy to live in Paul's days, glad to listen to so simple and plain a teacher.

Galatians 4:15-16. For I bear you record, that, if it had been possible, ye would have plucked out your own eyes, and have given them to me. Am I therefore become your enemy, because I tell you the truth?

Ah! there are many who have incurred enmity through speaking the gospel very plainly, for the natural tendency of man is towards ceremony, towards some form of legal righteousness: he must have something aesthetic, something that delights his sensuous nature, something that he can see and hear, to mix up that with the simplicity of faith; and Paul was as clear as noonday against everything of that kind, and so the Galatians got at last to be angry with him. Well, he could not help that, but it did grieve him.

Galatians 4:17. They zealously affect you, but not well; yea, they would exclude you, that ye might affect them.

They would, if they could, turn you out of our love that you might run after them. These false teachers would shut us out of your hearts that your hearts might go after them.

Galatians 4:18-21. But it is good to be zealously affected always in a good thing, and not only when I am present with you. My little children, of whom I travail in birth again until Christ be formed in you. I desire to be present with you now, and to change my voice; for I stand in doubt of you. Tell me, ye that desire to be under the law, do ye not hear the law?

Will you not listen to what the law itself teaches? Here is a little bit from one of its first books, the book of Genesis.

Galatians 4:22-23. For it is written, that Abraham had two sons, the one by a bondmaid, and the other by a freewoman. But he who was of the bondwoman was born after the flesh;

In the strength of Abraham.

Galatians 4:23. But he of the freewoman was by promise.

In the power of God, born after both father and mother had ceased to be capable of becoming parents, born in the power of God.

Galatians 4:24. Which things are an allegory: for these are the two covenants: the one from the mount Sinai, which gendereth to bondage, which is Hagar.

Those that are under the law are the children, therefore, of the bondwoman: they are born slaves.

Galatians 4:25. For this Hagar is mount Sinai in Arabia, and answereth to Jerusalem which now is, and is in bondage with her children.

It is old Judaism coming from Sinai, "This do, and thou shalt live," and all the children that are born under it are children of nature, and they are not the children of promise.

Galatians 4:26. But Jerusalem which is above is free, which is the mother of us all.

This is Sarah, and they that believe are the Isaac-children, the children of holy laughter, born according to the power of God.

Galatians 4:27-29. For it is written, Rejoice, thou barren that bearest not: break forth and cry, thou that travailest not: for the desolate hath many more children than she which hath an husband, Now we, brethren, as Isaac was, are the children of promise. But as then he that was born after the flesh persecuted him that was born after the Spirit, even so it is now.

The child of Hagar could not hear the child of Sarah, and they that seek salvation by the works of the law, and by outward ceremonies, cannot endure the children of faith.

Galatians 4:30-31. Nevertheless what saith the scripture? Cast out the bondwoman and her son; for the son of the bondwoman shall not be heir with the son of the freewoman. So then, brethren, we are not children of the bondwoman, but of the free.

This exposition consisted of readings from Galatians 4:12-31; Galatians 5:1-4; Galatians 5:19-26; Galatians 6:1-11.

Galatians Chapter 5

Verses 1-26

Galatians 5:1-4. Stand fast therefore in the liberty wherewith Christ had made us free, and be not entangled again with the yoke of bondage. Behold, I Paul say unto you, that if ye be circumcised, Christ shall profit you nothing. For I testify again to every man that is circumcised, that he is a debtor to do the whole law. Christ is become of no effect unto you whosoever of you are justified by the law; ye are fallen from grace.

If you mean to have anything to with salvation by works, get you gone; you are the children of the bond-woman.

Galatians 5:19-21. Now the works of the flesh are manifest, which are these: Adultery, fornication, uncleanness, lasciviousness, Idolatry, witchcraft, hatred, variance, emulations, wrath, strife, seditions, heresies, Envyings, murders, drunkenness, reveling, and such like:

A black catalogue, but sin is very prolific. We must take care that we avoid each one of these works of the flesh, or else we shall give no proof that we are led by the Spirit of God and possess the grace of God.

Galatians 5:21. Of the which I tell you before, as I have also told you in time past, that they which do such things shall not inherit the kingdom of God.

Read over the list. Put the question to conscience, "Am I guilty of such things?" If so, do not suppose that the holding of orthodox doctrine will save you, or that any kind of religious ceremony will save you. You must be delivered from these lusts of the flesh — these deeds of the flesh, or you cannot inherit the kingdom of God.

Galatians 5:22-23. But the fruit of the spirit is love, joy, peace, longsuffering, gentleness, goodness, faith, meekness, temperance: against such there is no law.

Surely, neither human nor divine. These are things which are commended on all hands. But if we do not have them — if they are not found in us —then we have not the Spirit, for if we had the Spirit, we should boast the fruit of the Spirit.

Galatians 5:24-26. And they that are Christ's have crucified the flesh with the affections and lusts. If we live in the Spirit, let us also walk in the Spirit. Let us not be desirous of vain glory,

A very common sin — wishing to shine. Whether we deserve to be honoured or not, still wanting to be fore-horse in the team, and to take the leading place. "Let us not be desirous of vain glory."

Galatians 5:26. Provoking one another, envying one another.

If each would strive who should do the greatest deeds of love, and each were willing to take the lowest place, then this evil would never be known again.

This exposition consisted of readings from Galatians 4:12-31; Galatians 5:1-4; Galatians 5:19-26; Galatians 6:1-11.

Verses 13-26

Galatians 5:13. For, brethren, ye have been called unto liberty; only use not liberty for an occasion to the flesh, but by love serve one another.

Do not turn your liberty into license. The apostle, in this Epistle, had began urging the Christians of Galatians to stand fast in the liberty wherewith Christ had made them free, and never to be again entangled with the yoke of legal bondage. He warned them against that error into which many have fallen. But you know that it is often our tendency, if we escape from one error, to rush into another. So the apostle guards these Christian against that Antinomian spirit which teaches us that freedom from the law allows indulgence in sin: "Use not your liberty for an occasion to the flesh, but by love serve one another."

Galatians 5:14. For all the law is fulfilled in one word, even in this; Thou shalt love thy neighbor as thyself.

Oh, if that "one word" were so engraven on our hearts as to influence all our lives, what blessed lives of love to God and love to men we should lead!

Galatians 5:15. But if ye bite and devour one another, take heed that ye be not consumed one of another.

When dogs and wolves bite one another, it is according to their nature; but it is bad indeed when sheep take to biting one another. If I must be bitten at all, let me rather be bitten by a dog than by a sheep. That is to say, the wounds inflicted by the godly are far more painful to bear, and last much longer, than those caused by wicked men. Besides, we can say with the psalmist, "It was not an enemy that reproached me; then I could have borne it." It is natural that the serpent's seed should nibble at our heel, and seek to do us injury; but when the bite comes from a brother, — from a child of God, then it is peculiarly painful. Well might the apostle write, "If ye bite and devour one another, take heed that ye be not consumed one of another." I have lived long enough to see churches absolutely destroyed, not by any external attacks, but by internal contention.

34

Galatians 5:16. This I say then, walk in the Spirit, and ye shall not fulfill the lust of the flesh.

If your life is guided by the Spirit of God, — if you are spiritual men, and your actions are wrought in the power of the Spirit, "ye shall not fulfill the lust of the flesh."

Galatians 5:17. For the flesh lusteth against the Spirit, and the Spirit against the flesh:

They will never agree; these two powers are always contrary one to the other. If you think that you can help God by getting angry, you make a great mistake. You cannot fight God's battles with the devil's weapons. It is not possible that the power of the flesh should help the power of the Spirit.

Galatians 5:17-18. And these are contrary the one to the other: so that ye cannot do the things that ye would. But if ye be led of the Spirit, ye are not under the law.

The law is ever to you the blessed rule by which you judge your conduct, but it is not a law of condemnation to you, neither are you seeking salvation by it.

Galatians 5:19-21. Now the works of the flesh are manifest, which are these; adultery, fornication, uncleanness, lasciviousness, idolatry, witchcraft, hatred, variance, emulations, wrath, strife, seditions, heresies, envyings, murders, drunkenness, revellings, and such like:

The list is always too long to be completed; we are obliged to sum up with a kind of et cetera: "and such like."

Galatians 5:21. Of the which I tell you before, as I have also told you in time past, that they which do such things shall not inherit the kingdom of God.

A very solemn, searching, sweeping declaration. Let each man judge himself by this test. "The fruit of the Spirit" — is equally manifest, as the apostle goes on to say,

Galatians 5:22-23. But the fruit of the Spirit is love, joy, peace, longsuffering, gentleness, goodness, faith, meekness, temperance: against such there is no law.

Neither human nor divine. Good men make no law against these things, nor does God, for he approves of them. What a wonderful cluster of the grapes of Eshcol we have here! "The fruit of the Spirit" — as if all this were but one after all; — many luscious berries forming one great cluster. Oh, that all these things may be in us and abound, that we may be neither barren nor unfruitful!

Galatians 5:24. And they that are Christ's have crucified the flesh with the affections and lusts.

It is not yet dead, but it is crucified. It hangs up on the cross, straining to break away from the iron hold fast, but it cannot, for it is doomed to die. Happy indeed shall that day be when it shall be wholly dead.

Galatians 5:25-26. If we live in the Spirit, let us also walk in the spirit. Let us not be desirous of vain glory, provoking one another, envying one another.

Do Christian people need to be talked to like this? Ay, that they do, for the best of men are but men at their best, and the godliest saint is liable to fall into the fondest sin unless the grace of God prevent. Oh, that we could expel from the Church of Christ all vain glorying, all provoking of one another, and all envying of one another! How often, if one Christian brother does a little more than his fellow-workers, they begin to find fault with him; and if one is blessed with greater success than others are, how frequently that success is disparaged and spoken of slightingly! This spirit of envy is, more or less, in us all; and though, perhaps we are not exhibiting it just now, it only needs a suitable opportunity for its display, and it would be manifested. No man here has any idea of how bad he really is. You do not know how good the grace of God can make you, nor how bad you are by nature, nor how bad you might become if that nature were left to itself.

This exposition consisted of readings from Galatians 5:13-26; and Galatians 6:1-2.

Galatians Chapter 6

Verse 1-2

Galatians 6:1. Brethren, if a man be overtaken in a fault, —

If he travels so slowly that his faults catch him up, and knock him down: "If a man be overtaken in a fault," —

Galatians 6:1. Ye which are spiritual, restore such an one in the spirit of meekness;

Set his bones for him if they have been broken; put him in his proper place again.

Galatians 6:1. Considering thyself, lest thou also be tempted.

What would you wish others to do to you if you were in the position of this fallen one? The apostle does not say, "Considering thyself lest thou also be overtaken in a fault." No, but, "lest thou also be tempted," — as much as to say, "It only needs the temptation to come to you, and you will yield to it."

Galatians 6:2. Bear ye one another's burdens, and fulfill the law of Christ.

This exposition consisted of readings from Galatians 5:13-26; and Galatians 6:1-2.

Verses 1-10

Galatians 6:1. Brethren, if a man be overtaken in a fault,—

He is a slow traveler; he is not speeding swiftly on the way to heaven, so the fault overtakes him. Had he been quicker of pace, he might have outstripped it; but he is "overtaken in a fault." What then? Turn him out of the church? Have done with him? No. "If a man be overtaken in a fault,"—

Galatians 6:1. Ye which are spiritual, restore such an one in the spirit of meekness;

Pick him up, help him to run better than he did before.

Galatians 6:1. Considering thyself, lest thou also be tempted.

Paul does not say, "Lest thou also fall;" but, "Lest thou also be tempted," — as much as to say, "You will be sure to fall if you are tempted;" and that man, who thinks that other people ought to be cast off because they have committed a fault, is so proud in his own heart that he only needs to be tempted, and he would fall, too. This is a very expressive way of putting the matter: "Considering thyself, lest thou also be tempted."

Galatians 6:2. Bear ye one another's burdens, and so fulfill the law of Christ.

Help your brethren. If you see that they have more to do than they can accomplish, take a share of their labour. If they have a heavier burden than they can bear, try to put your shoulder beneath their load, and so lighten it for them.

Galatians 6:3. For if a man think himself to be something, when he is nothing, he deceiveth himself.

Paul does not say, "He deceiveth other people;" no, "he deceiveth himself." As a general rule, other people find him out, they learn what he really is, but "he deceiveth himself."

Galatians 6:4-5. But let every man prove his own work, and then shall he have rejoicing in himself alone, and not in another. For every man shall bear his own burden.

There is, after all, a burden which we cannot carry for others, and which we cannot shift upon others. There are burdens of care, and sorrow, and trouble, which we can take from other men's shoulders; but the great burden of responsibility before God, each man must himself carry.

Galatians 6:6. Let him that is taught in the word communicate unto him that teacheth in all good things.

Those who are taught, should maintain those who are their teachers as far as they are able to do so.

Galatians 6:7. Be not deceived; God is not mocked: for whatsoever a man soweth, that shall he also reap.

That is true under the gospel as well as under the law.

Galatians 6:8. For he that soweth to his flesh shall of the flesh reap corruption;

That is what always comes to the flesh; it decays and corrupts.

Galatians 6:8. But he that soweth to the Spirit shall of the Spirit reap life everlasting.

No corruption shall come to that which belongs to the Spirit: "He that soweth to the Spirit shall of the Spirit reap life everlasting."

Galatians 6:9-10. And let us not be weary in well doing: for in due season are shall reap, if we faint not. As we have therefore opportunity, let us do good unto all men, especially unto them who are if the household of faith.

This exposition consisted of readings from Galatians 5:13-26; and Galatians 6:1-10.

Verses 1-11

Galatians 6:1. Brethren, if a man be overtaken in a fault, ye which are spiritual, restore such an one in the spirit of meekness; considering thyself, lest thou also be tempted.

When Christians fall into a fault, it is on account of their traveling slowly on the road to heaven. Hence the expression, "If he be overtaken with a fault." He would not have been overtaken if he had been traveling faster. If his heart had been quick in the ways of the Lord, he would have outstripped the temptation. Now, when a brother falls into sin, it is too often the habit to push him down — to cast him out and forget him. But spiritually-minded persons must not do so. We must seek the restoration of the brother. Is there not more joy over the sheep that was lost than over those that went not astray? Have we not the best reason to deal tenderly with wanderers, since we cannot tell that we may not need the same generous offices for ourselves? "Considering thyself lest thou also be tempted." He seems to take it for granted that we probably should, if we were tempted as the other brother was.

Galatians 6:2. Bear ye one another's burdens, and so fulfill the law of Christ.

Help each other. If you have a light load. take a part of somebody else's.

Galatians 6:3. For if a man think himself to be something, when he is nothing, he deceiveth himself.

Mainly deceives himself. Other people generally find it out. It is no use estimating your fortune at so many millions, for it will not make it so; and it is of no use estimating yourself at a very high price, because it does not make it so. "He deceiveth himself."

Galatians 6:4-5. But let every man prove his own work, and then, shall he have rejoicing in himself alone, and not in another. For every man shall bear his own burden.

There are burdens of care and sorrow which we can help others to bear; but the burdens of responsibility each man must carry for himself. The load of service for the Master must be carried personally; and let us be glad to

41

shoulder it, since Christ has done so much for us. And how else can we express gratitude but by serving him?

Galatians 6:6. Let him that is taught in the word communicate unto him that teacheth in all good things.

If he gives you spirituals, do not suffer him to lack for temporals.

Galatians 6:7-8. Be not deceived: God is not mocked: for whatsoever a man soweth, that shall he also reap. For he that soweth to his flesh shall of the flesh reap

What the flesh always comes to by-and-bye.

Galatians 6:8. Corruption; but he that soweth to the Spirit

By faith in Christ — by being led of the Spirit.

Galatians 6:8-10. Shall of the Spirit reap life everlasting. And let us not be weary in well doing: for in due season we shall reap, it we faint not. As we have therefore opportunity, let us do good unto all men, especially unto them who are of the household of faith.

They have a first claim upon us. They are nearest of kin. They are our brethren in Christ. Let them have a Benjamin's portion.

Galatians 6:11. Ye see how large a letter I have written unto you with mine own hand.

Paul did not often write his own epistles. It is thought that he had a defect of the eyes. He employed an amanuensis generally. When he did write, he wrote generally in great capitals. I suppose that is what he meant. "You see how emphatic my writing is — what great characters I have made in writing to you." Or he may have meant that for a letter, written by him, this was a lengthy one.

This exposition consisted of readings from Galatians 4:12-31; Galatians 5:1-4; Galatians 5:19-26; Galatians 6:1-11.

Verses 6-18

Galatians 6:6-7. Let him that is taught in the word communicate unto him that teacheth in all good things. Be not deceived; God is not mocked: for whatsoever a man soweth, that shall he also reap.

Paul puts that in connection with the support of those who are teachers of the truth, and I have sometimes thought that, in certain churches where God's ministers have been starved, it was not very wonderful that the people should be starved, too. They thought so little about the pastor that they left him in need, so it was not strange that, as they sowed little, they reaped little. One of these misers said that his religion did not cost him more than a shilling a year, and somebody replied that he thought it was a shilling wasted on a bad thing, for his poor religion was not worth even that small amount.

Galatians 6:8. For he that soweth to his flesh shall of the flesh reap corruption;

He shall reap what flesh turns to in due time: "he shall of the flesh reap corruption." What is the end of flesh? The fairest flesh, that ever was moulded from the most beauteous form, ends in corruption; and if we live for the flesh, and sow to it, we shall reap "corruption."

Galatians 6:8. But he that soweth to the Spirit shall of the spirit reap life everlasting.

He shall reap what the Spirit really is, and what the Spirit really generates: "life everlasting." Of course, if a man sows tares, he reaps tares. If he sows wheat, he reaps wheat. If we sow to the flesh, we reap corruption. If we sow to the Spirit, we shall "reap life everlasting."

Galatians 6:9. And let us not be weary in well doing: for in due season we shall reap, if we faint not.

It is a pity to faint just when the time is coming to reap; so, sow on, brother and sister, sow on!

Galatians 6:10. As we have therefore opportunity, let us do good unto all men, especially unto them who are of the household of faith.

Extend your love, your charity, to all mankind; but let the center of that circle be in the home where God has placed you, — in the home of his people: "especially unto them who are of the household of faith."

Galatians 6:11. Ye see how large a letter I have written unto you with mine own hand.

I suppose that he meant, "See what big characters I have made. My eyes are weak, and so, when I do write a letter," says Paul, "in the dimness of this dungeon, with my poor weak eyes, and my hands fettered, I have to write text-hand, and give it to you in large letters. Well," he says, "then carry it out in big letters. You see with what large letters I have written to you, now emphasize it all, take it as emphatic, and carry it out with great diligence. As I have written this with mine own hand, and not used an amanuensis, I beseech you to pay the more attention to it, you Galatians, who seem to be so bewitched that, to deliver you from false doctrine, and an evil spirit, I would even write a letter with my own blood if it were needful."

Galatians 6:12-13. As many as desire to make a fair shew in the flesh, they constrain you to be circumcised; only lest they should suffer persecution for the cross of Christ. For neither they themselves who are circumcised keep the law; but desire to have you circumcised, that they may glory in your flesh.

"See," say they, "these Gentiles. We have converted them, and we have got them circumcised. Is not that a wonderful thing? "No, not at all, for he says,

Galatians 6:14. But God foretold that I should glory, save in the Cross of our Lord Jesus Christ, by whom the world is crucified unto me, and I unto the world.

"I have ceased to care", says Paul, "about glorying in men, and making other people glory in my converts. The world is dead to me, and I to it."

Galatians 6:15-17. For in Christ Jesus neither circumcision availeth any thing, nor uncircumcision, but a new creature. And as many as walk according to this rule, peace be on them, and mercy, and upon the Israel of God. From henceforth let no man trouble me: for I bear in my body the marks of the Lord Jesus.

I have the marks of the whips upon my body. I am the branded slave of Jesus Christ. There is no getting the marks out of me. I cannot run away. I cannot deny that he is my Master and my Owner: "I bear in my body the marks of the Lord Jesus'.

Galatians 6:18. Brethren, the grace of our Lord Jesus Christ be with your spirit. Amen.

And that is our benediction to you. The Lord fulfill it to each one of you!

Thank You

Thank you for purchasing this book. We truly value your custom. This book was put together to provide you with a collection of good commentary resources on the books of the Bible. It is our prayerful hope that God might use this work for His own glory and sovereign will.

We would be delighted to hear from you and received any messages, suggestions or corrections. You can contact us at:

expansivecommentarycollection@gmail.com

It is our promise that you email address will not be added to any mailing list or used for any purpose other than to communicate regarding this commentary series.

We trust that the Lord will continue to bless you as you live for Him.

Printed in Great Britain
by Amazon

81642521R00027